YOU CHO
BO

D0195743

COULD YOU ESCAPE THE PARIS CATACOMBS?

AN INTERACTIVE SURVIVAL ADVENTURE

BY MATT DOEDEN

CAPSTONE PRESS
a capstone imprint

You Choose Books are published by Capstone Press
1710 Roe Crest Drive, North Mankato, Minnesota 56003
www.capstonepub.com

Library of Congress Cataloging-in-Publication Data
Names: Doeden, Matt, author.
Title: Could you escape the Paris catacombs? : an interactive survival
  adventure / by Matt Doeden.
Description: North Mankato, Minnesota : Capstone Press, [2020] | Series: You
  choose: can you escape? | Summary: Your survival depends on making the
  right choices at key moments when you are lost in the catacombs of Paris.
Identifiers: LCCN 2019008531| ISBN 9781543573947 (hardcover) | ISBN
  9781543575620 (paperback) | ISBN 9781543573985 (ebook pdf)
Subjects: LCSH: Plot-your-own stories. | CYAC: Catacombs—Fiction. |
  Survival—Fiction. | Plot-your-own stories. | Paris (France)—Fiction. |
  France—Fiction.
Classification: LCC PZ7.D692 Co 2020 | DDC [Fic]—dc23
LC record available at https://lccn.loc.gov/2019008531

Editorial Credits
Mari Bolte, editor; Bobbie Nuytten, designer; Eric Gohl, media researcher:
Laura Manthe, premedia specialist

Photo Credits
Alamy: Album, 92, Edward Westmacott, 36, Hemis, 46; Bridgeman Images:
Archives Charmet/Bibliotheque des Arts Decoratifs, Paris, France, 10, Bibliotheque
Nationale, Paris, France, 85, Photo © The Holbarn Archive, 80, Sputnik/State Russian
Museum, St. Petersburg, Russia, 34; Capstone: 4; Newscom: akg-images, 16, SIPA/
Eric Beracassat, 50; Shutterstock: Alex Guevara, 22, Andrea Izzotti, 6, 89, 105,
FrimuFilms, 29, Ilias Kouroudis, cover (tunnel), back cover, javarman, 76, Novikov
Aleksey, 61, Ravenash, 56, Stas Guk, 71, 72, Steven Bostock, cover (skulls), Viacheslav
Lopatin, 42; SuperStock: age fotostock/Javier Marina, 102, Photononstop, 98

Printed and bound in the United States of America.
PA70

TABLE OF CONTENTS

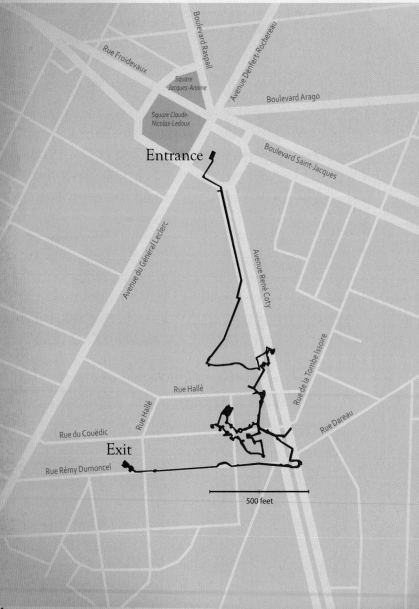

ABOUT YOUR ADVENTURE

YOU are deep below the streets of Paris, France, in the twisting network of tunnels known as the Paris Catacombs. It's dark and damp. Every footfall echoes off of the cracked walls. Skulls grin at you as your flashlight begins to flicker. Your heart races at the thought of the darkness closing in around you.

A small portion of the tunnels are open to the public. But you went off the grid, in search of the unknown. Can you escape the wild, unmapped depths of the Paris Catacombs? Your choices will guide the story. Will you backtrack or delve deeper? Will you scream for help? Will anyone hear you if you do? Can you find a way out—or will you join the others as a permanent part of the catacombs?

Turn the page to begin your adventure.

Chapter 1

THE CATACOMBS CALL

You've landed in Paris. The city is full of life. People pass you as you stroll down the streets, speaking animatedly to friends or just enjoying the bright sun and fresh air. You're surrounded by historical sites and modern-day marvels. This trip is a dream come true.

But, even here in the open street full of wonder, there's a part of the city you can't stop thinking about. You've heard of this place, but only in whispers. The mystery sparked your interest from the first mention. You've thought about going there and seeing things for yourself for years. You can't miss this opportunity. The Paris Catacombs are calling you from below.

Turn the page.

The underground tunnels, resting place to six million dead, are not a secret, but the air of mystery surrounds them. It's another world and largely unmapped. It's a frontier . . . a massive grave . . . a historical monument. It fills you with equal parts terror and wonder. "Don't go down there alone," people warn. "You may never return." Yet you cannot shake the urge to see it for yourself.

Your footsteps quicken as you start to move through the streets with a purpose. You have to go. You have to explore for yourself. An opening stands before you. The catacombs lie beyond. A trickle of sunlight spills into the opening. It creates a narrow shaft of light that dims, then fades away into pitch blackness. You can hear the distant dripping of water and a low, creaky scraping sound.

You take a breath and step forward into the darkness. A wave of cool, damp air sweeps over you. You pause, waiting for your eyes to adjust to the darkness. "This is it," you whisper. You take another step, then another. You have entered the Catacombs of Paris.

To see the catacombs as a young worker in the late 1700s, turn to page 11.

To explore the catacombs as a modern-day tourist, turn to page 37.

To help rescue of a group of teens lost in the labyrinth, turn to page 77.

Chapter 2

NIGHT SHIFT

The first thing that hits you is the smell. Even before you step foot inside the catacombs, the powerful odor of death and decay is evident. It's almost enough to make you turn around.

"Don't worry," says Luc. This is your first day on the job, but Luc has been doing it for a week. "You'll get used to it. I think I turned about four shades of green on my first day, but now I barely notice it."

It's 1785, and you're a teenager trying to make your way in Paris, one of the greatest cities in the world. It's a strange and fascinating time. The city's graveyards are filled beyond capacity.

Turn the page.

Local authorities have decided that the graveyards will be emptied. The remains of countless millions will be moved to an ancient series of mining tunnels that lie below the city's streets. You've taken a lot of odd jobs since you came to Paris a year ago. But this is by far the strangest.

"It's not a complicated job," Luc explains to you. "Workers above ground dig up the bodies from the old Holy Innocents cemetery. They dump them down a well that leads into the quarry—that's the part of the catacombs where we'll be working. We just stack the bones down below. Simple."

A shudder runs down your spine. "OK, but isn't all of this spooky enough? Why do we only work at night?"

Luc laughs. "I wondered the same thing. But then I thought about it. How do you think the fine, upstanding citizens of Paris would feel about this project? They want to pretend not to know. So we work at night. That way, we don't get so many complaints."

As you make your way down deeper into the quarries, the horror of the situation strikes you. The path is lit with flickering torches and lanterns. The piles of remains seem even creepier.

Workers are stacking bodies onto carts. Then they pile them high along the walls of the quarry's large chambers. The bodies are in various stages of decay. Some of the bones are a thousand years old and browned with age. Eyeless skulls stare at you from every angle.

Turn the page.

The smell is more concentrated here in the tunnels. It makes you retch. When Luc first told you about this job, it sounded interesting. Now it feels like you signed up for a horror story.

"You two, get back to work!" An older, balding man approaches you. "We have corpses coming in by the thousands tonight. I want them stacked on that far wall. Get to it!"

You and Luc work as a team loading the dead onto carts. Some of them are very old. They're nothing but bones wrapped in rags. Others aren't fully decayed yet. Those are the ones that really make your stomach churn. You load and wheel one cart after another. As Luc grabs the feet of yet another body, you grab under the shoulders. You heave it onto a pile. It lands with a sickening crunch. It's all too much.

"I'm going to vomit," you say.

"Don't do it in here!" Luc replies. He points to a nearby passageway. "Go down there. The smell is already unbearable in here. We don't need to add vomit to it."

You put one hand over your mouth while holding a torch in the other. You rush down the tunnel. You don't want to let the other workers hear you heaving, so you follow the tunnel until you're far from earshot. You drop to your hands and knees.

When you're done, you feel dizzy. Your head is swimming, and your stomach is still churning. You should get back before you get in trouble for slacking off. But you fear that if you stand up, you might faint or throw up again.

To get up and go back to work, turn to page 16.
To rest here for a few minutes, turn to page 18.

It's your first day on the job. You've got to get back. Using one arm to brace yourself against the cold wall, you rise to your feet. Immediately, the world begins to spin. Before you realize what's happening, you black out. Your body collapses to the hard stone floor.

Most of the catacombs are more than 100 feet (30.5 meters) below street level.

When you wake up, everything feels fuzzy. You don't know how long you were unconscious. Your torch lies beside you, just barely burning. If it goes out, you'll be in total darkness. You have to get back to the main chamber—now!

You look around. You're at an intersection of tunnels. Which one did you take to get down here? You were in such a rush that you weren't paying much attention. And now the knock on your head has you feeling confused and sluggish.

"Was it that way?" you mumble to yourself, peering down into the darkness. "Yes . . . yes. That way. I think it was that way."

Your torch flickers. The flame is almost out. If you stay still and call for help, the light will last longer. But what if no one hears?

To stay where you are and yell for help, turn to page 19.
To grab the torch and start running, turn to page 24.

You just need a minute or two to catch your breath. The smell in the side tunnel is not as bad as the larger chamber. You sit for a moment to let your turning stomach settle.

That's when something catches your eye. It's a faint orange glow coming from farther down the tunnel. It looks like torchlight, and it appears to be moving. Who would be down here? None of the workers would have a reason to be that deep in the catacombs. And no one else is allowed down here at night.

To investigate the light, turn to page 20.
To return to work, turn to page 21.

"Luc!" you shout. Your voice echoes off of the tunnel walls. "Anyone?"

It takes a few moments before you see a torchlight. To your relief, it's Luc.

"I was just about to give up on you," he says. "I was wheeling the cart back when I heard you call. Feeling better?" He helps you to your feet. "Don't worry, it's happened to all of us."

Luc leads you back to the main part of the quarry. You've got to get back to work if you want to keep your job. There's no time to waste.

Turn to page 21.

Your curiosity gets the best of you. You pick yourself up and start down the tunnel in the direction of the torchlight. You're heading away from the quarry. But as long as you don't take any turns, you feel confident that you can find your way back.

You follow the winding tunnel. The torchlight grows steadily brighter. Finally, you catch up to it.

It's a man holding the torch. He doesn't seem surprised to see you, which seems a little odd.

"I'm Phil," he says. "Come now, the treasure is near. Are you going to help me find it?"

"Treasure?" you ask, confused. "What treasure?"

Phil doesn't seem to hear you. "Come!" he snaps, walking farther down the tunnel. "It's close now. I've never been so close. Let's go!"

To decline Phil's offer, turn to page 23.
To join Phil and search for treasure, turn to page 26.

While you've been sick in the tunnels, the others have been working hard. Some noticed your absence, so you jump right in to help. Stacking the bones still makes you feel ill, but it's not quite as bad as before. Maybe Luc is right. Maybe with time, you'll be able to forget that you're touching corpses.

While some workers just stack remains, others have started crafting the bones into works of art. They carefully arrange them against the walls and into structures. Some start calling this decorated area the ossuary. The ossuary would be beautiful if it wasn't made from human remains.

Night after night, you return to the catacombs. The dead pile grows higher and higher. Millions of bones line the walls.

Turn the page.

The catacomb's tunnels were created when limestone was mined to build the city in as early as the 14th century.

Months later, you're busy at work when you hear that a man is missing. Someone wandered too far into the tunnels and hasn't returned. You flash back to your first day on the job and the terror you felt alone in the dark. You shudder thinking about someone else lost in those tunnels.

To go search for the missing man, turn to page 32.
To stay put and keep working, turn to page 35.

You watch as Phil disappears around a corner. What were you thinking coming down here? Who follows a stranger into the dark? It's time to get back to reality.

You turn to make your way back to the large chamber. But there are so many paths to choose from. What seemed like a straight walk in one direction feels quite different now. How do you get back? You glance at your torch. It's still burning strong, but it won't last forever.

You follow the tunnel that you think is the way out. After a while, you wonder how long you've been walking. It seems like a long time. Did you go the wrong way? Panic begins to set in. If you're lost, there's probably no hope for you. No one—except Phil—knows where you are.

To turn around and try a different tunnel, turn to page 28.
To continue along this tunnel, turn to page 30.

The thought of being trapped down here in the dark is terrifying. You have to go, and you have to go *now*. You pick yourself up and start down the closest tunnel. You start at a brisk walk, but soon you are running.

You round a bend, then another. Nothing looks familiar. You've gone too far. Or—not far enough? This can't be the right tunnel!

You spin around and start in the other direction. Maybe you missed a path. You turn so fast that the torch flickers. Then it dies. You are left in total darkness. You freeze in your tracks, looking for any faint glow of light. You listen for any sound. There's nothing. There's only darkness and silence.

"Help!" you shout. "Anyone! Help me, please!"

The only sound you hear is the echo of your own voice.

Luc probably thinks you gave up and went home. Nobody is going to come looking for you. All you can do is blindly roam the tunnels, hoping to see some light or hear a voice. But in the twisting tunnels of the Paris Catacombs, you know that your odds aren't very good.

THE END

To follow another path, turn to page 9.
To learn more about the Paris Catacombs, turn to page 103.

The word "treasure" catches your interest. What could be more exciting than a treasure hunt? If you found a huge stack of gold, you'd never have to have a horrible job again.

Forgetting Luc and basic common sense, you charge off after Phil. He leads you on a winding path through the catacombs. At times it feels like you're walking in circles, but Phil says he can sense that the treasure is close.

"Any moment now," he mumbles, holding his torch out in front of him. "I can smell it. Can you smell it? It's close."

You trek deeper and deeper into the tunnels. The endless twists and turns make you feel dizzy. Finally, Phil lets out a squeal and takes off running. "It's here! It's here!"

He's surprisingly quick. You do your best to keep up, but you're quickly losing ground. Phil disappears around a corner. By the time you reach it, his light is nowhere to be seen.

You're all alone, deep in the catacombs of Paris. It's cold and damp. And your torch just burned out.

Maybe searching for treasure wasn't your best idea. You wish you could go back in time and make a different choice.

THE END

To follow another path, turn to page 9.
To learn more about the Paris Catacombs, turn to page 103.

Your heart is racing. Everything looks the same! You spin around, looking frantically in both directions. You must have come the wrong way. This can't be right!

You sprint back the way you came, arriving at an intersection of tunnels. Do you go left or right? Your torch flickers. It won't keep burning for much longer. You pick a tunnel and start to run. The thunderous clop-clop of your boots on the stone floor is the only sound you can hear.

Suddenly the floor falls away to nothing. In your panic, you didn't realize that the tunnel opened up into a large mine shaft. You flail your arms. Your fingers grab at the side of the wall, but there's nothing to hold on to. You fall through the open shaft.

Rocks and minerals, including limestone, gypsum, and chalk, were mined from under the city. The Louvre was built with Parisian limestone.

You don't know when you'll hit the bottom. The fall into the darkness seems to take an eternity. You realize that the last thing you will ever see is the faint flickering light of your torch as it hits the stone floor.

THE END

To follow another path, turn to page 9.
To learn more about the Paris Catacombs, turn to page 103.

Just a little farther, you tell yourself. *The way out is straight ahead.* You hope you're right. You know that you're betting with your life. You press forward through the narrow tunnel. Water drips from cracks in the walls. Your torch begins to flicker and dim.

"This is wrong," you say out loud. "What have I done?"

Then you smell it. It's the smell of death. There's a dim glow of light ahead. You quicken your pace and burst out into the main chamber. You never thought you'd be so glad to smell and see thousands of corpses piled together.

"You there," shouts the balding man. "Get back to work!"

You smile and shake your head. "Sorry, I quit," you announce.

You'll apologize to Luc later. Right now, all that matters is getting back above ground. You'll find some other job. You'll have to. You're never stepping foot down here again.

THE END

To follow another path, turn to page 9.
To learn more about the Paris Catacombs, turn to page 103.

You still have nightmares about your first day in the catacombs. You wouldn't wish that on anyone. You're the first to volunteer to search for the missing man. Luc is right behind you. The two of you form a team. Several other men pair up into teams as well.

Luc leads the way down a narrow tunnel. It branches off several times. "I went down this way," he says. "Once. And I didn't go very far. It's very tight and there's loose rock everywhere. But we ought to at least check it out. Watch your footing."

You're just barely able to squeeze through the passageway, which seems more like a crack in the rock than a proper tunnel. You each carry a torch. In the tight quarters, it glows right in your eyes, temporarily blinding you.

As you emerge from one snug section, you spot something ahead. It's the missing man! He's lying on the ground, bleeding from a wound on his head. You call to Luc, and rush over to help.

"He must have bumped his head going through that narrow part," Luc says, looking back the way you came. You peel off your outer shirt and wrap it around the man's wound. He's conscious now, but very groggy.

"What were you doing?" you ask.

"Ghosts. I saw ghosts," the man answers, dazed. "They told me to follow them." That doesn't make any sense to you. You wonder what he really saw. Tales of the dead haunting this place are common, but you've never heard of anyone actually seeing them.

Turn the page.

"I think you've been down here too long, friend," Luc says as he helps the man to his feet. You couldn't agree more. Once you get this worker back to safety, it will be time for you to leave as well. You don't want to be the next one chasing ghosts in the catacombs.

The idea of ghost sightings are popular among those seeking a paranormal experience in the catacombs.

THE END

To follow another path, turn to page 9.
To learn more about the Paris Catacombs, turn to page 103.

You back into a shadow and stand as quietly as you can. Luckily, no one notices you. Several others volunteer to go searching for the missing man. You wish you could help, but you just can't make yourself go into the tunnels again. Once is enough.

The search parties find no trace of the man. He's just . . . gone. With a shudder, you realize that could easily have been you. The catacombs of Paris are no place for adventure. You'll just keep doing your work. There are millions of dead that still need to be stacked.

THE END

To follow another path, turn to page 9.
To learn more about the Paris Catacombs, turn to page 103.

Chapter 3

INTO THE DEPTHS

"Oh look, it's another painting!" says Tonya, rolling her eyes. You playfully tap your older sister on the arm. She's not a fan of art like you and your parents are, and you know she's bored.

"Cut it out," you say. "Mom and Dad have been dreaming about this trip since they were kids."

You do have to admit that art museums are starting to lose their appeal. This is the fifth one you've been to this week. It's not that you don't enjoy seeing classic works of art. But there's more to Paris than da Vinci and Michelangelo.

Your parents stand in front of another painting, deep in thought. They could stare at the same painting for an hour.

Turn the page.

"Come on," you say, dragging Tonya over to where they're standing. "Mom . . . Dad," you begin. They don't even hear you. You clear your throat loudly. "Mom!"

Your mom looks over. "Hmm?" she says.

"We're ready to go," you say. "Would it be OK if the two of us saw some of the city's sights? We could meet you back at the hotel later this evening."

Your mother gives you a long look. "Well, OK," she says. "But stay together. And be back by sunset." She turns back to the painting.

Tonya lets out a little yelp of joy, earning some stern looks from the museum's patrons. The two of you hurry outside. The sun is shining. It's a beautiful day. Three local teenagers stand on a street corner, talking and laughing. One of them waves you over.

"*Bonjour.* I'm Ines," says a girl with long, straight, black hair. "Did you like the museum?"

Tonya shrugs. "I've seen enough museums," she says. "We're looking to see something else."

Ines smiles. "What did you have in mind?"

Neither of you hesitates. You've talked about them since you found out about this trip. "The catacombs!" you blurt out at the same time.

Ines laughs as her friends gather around. "You could take a tour of the catacombs," she says. "It's a very safe—and legal—way to get a taste of them with the rest of the tourists." Ines winks.

One of the other teens laughs. He's a short boy with wire-rimmed glasses. "Or you can see them the fun way . . . with us!" He extends a hand. "I'm René. This is our friend Peter."

Turn the page.

"If you want to see the *real* catacombs, you've found the right people," Peter brags. "We go exploring there all the time."

"Wait," Tonya says, taking a step back. "I thought people weren't allowed to go down there at all, except with the tours."

Peter laughs. "Of course it's not really legal. But it's not like the catacombs police are down there waiting for us."

Tonya bites her lip. She's not the most adventurous person in the world. You can tell that the idea of breaking the rules is making her nervous. But it fills you with excitement. You just know that if Tonya gave it a chance, you could both have an experience that you'll never forget.

To go with Ines, René, and Peter, go to page 41.
To say no and go on an official tour of the catacombs, turn to page 44.

You know what Tonya is thinking, but this is just an offer you can't refuse. Ines, René, and Peter live here. You're sure they know what they're doing.

"Let's do it!" you blurt out before your sister has a chance to object.

Before heading down, the group stops to grab some gear—flashlights, extra batteries, and snacks. Then Peter leads the group down a dark alleyway. He points toward a manhole tucked against an old stone building.

"That's our way in," Peter says, kneeling down and moving the heavy metal manhole cover. "Not many people know about it. We *cataphiles* keep our entrances as secret as possible." One by one, you slip through the narrow opening and emerge into another world.

Turn the page.

Ines starts an app on her phone. "I use this to keep track of where we've been," she explains. "René is working on building a map of this section of the catacombs."

You walk a little ways on a downward slope. Soon, the only light you can see comes from your flashlights. Everyone has enough batteries for a couple of hours.

The ossuary is decorated with skulls and leg bones. Smaller bones are hidden behind the ossuary walls.

Tonya shivers. "It's cold down here," she says. Her voice sounds strange as it echoes off of the corridor walls. "And these tunnels are so tight."

You agree. You've never been claustrophobic. But down here, you can almost feel the weight of the rock and earth pressing down on you.

The tunnel branches off. "We explored that tunnel yesterday," Ines says, pointing to the left. "There are some cool things to see that way, if you're interested. Or we could go this way," she points to the right. "We haven't mapped any of that yet. We have no idea what we might find. It'll be an adventure!"

To go left and see what the group already discovered, turn to page 49.

To go right and help map a new area, turn to page 52.

The idea of sneaking down into the forbidden parts of the catacombs fills you with excitement. But you look over to see Tonya biting her fingernails—something she always does when she's scared. How much fun would it be if your sister is terrified the whole time? So with a sigh, you politely decline the invitation.

Ines shrugs. "No problem. I'm sure you'll really enjoy a tour. Even the tunnels you're allowed to see are pretty interesting. Have fun!"

"Thanks," you reply with a smile. Already, Tonya seems more at ease. She's not biting her nails anymore, and she looks relieved. "Let's go," you say, pulling her by the arm.

By the time you reach the official entrance to the catacombs, it's mid-afternoon. You barely make it in time for the day's final tour.

You and Tonya follow your guide, a young man named Louis, through the entrance. Half a dozen other tourists follow along behind.

"These were built in the 13th century," Louis explains. "The tunnels stretch for hundreds of miles. Many of the passages remain unmapped to this day. It's terribly dangerous to stray from the group. If you get lost down here, you might never find your way back."

You follow Louis through the winding tunnels. It's rough and slippery. You almost fall once. It's also chilly.

"I wish I'd brought a jacket," Tonya whispers. You agree. The sun may be shining above ground, but it's damp and cool down here.

"We're about to enter the ossuary," Louis says as you come upon a large chamber.

Turn the page.

The words *Arrête! C'est ici l'empire de la mort* are written above the entrance. Louis tells you it means, "Stop! Here lies the Empire of the Dead."

The ossuary takes your breath away. It's filled with bones. Piles of bones. Walls of bones. Thousands of neatly stacked skulls stare blankly at you.

The ossuary was officially named the Paris Municipal Ossuary in 1786.

Tonya grabs your arm. "This is creepy," she whispers.

It *is* creepy. *These were once people*, you think. And now their remains are being used as decorations. A part of you feels like it's wrong even to be here. But you can't look away.

"Look over here!" says one of the other tourists, a young woman named Sonja. She's found a tunnel that's blocked off. "It says we're not supposed to go this way, but I see a light down there!"

She's right. There's a soft, glowing light flickering from somewhere down the tunnel. The passageway is gated off, but the gate is not securely closed.

Turn the page.

You look around. Louis and the rest of the group are a little farther down in the tunnels. Louis is busy answering questions and not paying any attention to you. It would be easy to slip through and take a quick peek.

"Don't even think about it," Tonya says, biting her nails. "There's no way I'm going down there."

You grin. "I know you won't. But there's nothing stopping me."

Tonya shakes her head. "Are you crazy? There's plenty to see here without sneaking off. Let's just head back to the rest of the group."

To return to the group, turn to page 59.
To check out the blocked-off tunnel, turn to page 60.

"Show us what you found," you say, heading left. The tunnel forks off again and again, but Ines knows exactly where to go.

"When you've been down here enough, you get a good sense of direction," she says.

Puddles of water—some of them ankle-deep—cover the way. René laughs as Tonya carefully steps around them. "Don't bother," he says. "You're in the catacombs. You're going to get wet."

He's right. The air is damp and musty. The sound of dripping water is everywhere. Your shoes squish on the rock floor as you creep along. Even though you try to be careful where you step, your pants are soon soaked up to your knees.

Soon you come to a spot where the tunnel widens. "Check this out," Peter says, shining his light on one of the walls.

Turn the page.

You gasp. It's a painting! Life-sized skeletons and spirits adorn the walls. They're bright and vivid, captured forever by spray paint. You've seen hundreds of paintings already on your trip, but this one holds your eye in a new way.

"Creepy," Tonya says. She doesn't share your appreciation for the graffiti art.

The catacombs have their own "cave police" called cataflics. Their role is to protect and preserve the catacombs.

"We don't condone graffiti in the catacombs," René explains. "Cataphiles are supposed to keep them as they are. But it is cool, isn't it?"

Just then you hear a low groaning followed by a crunching sound.

"What was that?" Tonya asks.

Peter, René, and Ines look concerned. "That sounded like something collapsed," Ines says. "It doesn't happen often, but it does happen."

"Collapsed?" Tonya gasps. "I don't like the sound of that. We should turn around!"

René scoffs. "You two do what you want. The exit is straight down that way. We're going deeper."

To head back to the exit, turn to page 54.
To continue on your adventure, turn to page 56.

There's no question about what you want to do.

"Where's the fun without the adventure?" you ask. Ines gives you a big grin and leads the group down the passageway to the right.

But as the minutes tick by, all you see is more tunnel. "Everything looks the same," you say, disappointed.

"That's the danger," René answers. He holds up his phone. "And that's why these maps are so important. So many of these tunnels look the same. One wrong turn and you might never find your way out."

The tunnel has taken a sharp downward slope. The air smells damp.

"Look," Tonya says, shining her light ahead.

The tunnel floor dips into a black pool. To your surprise, Peter steps in. The dropoff is sharp. He is quickly knee-deep in the water. He turns and gives the group a smile.

"Good news, everyone," Peter says. "It looks like we get to take a swim!"

"You've got to be kidding me," Tonya says.

"It's all part of exploring," Peter replies. Ines is already putting everyone's phones into a waterproof pouch.

"Look," Peter says, pulling out a headlamp and putting it on. "Feel free to go back if you want. Otherwise, get ready to get wet."

You stare at the dark water. Was this really what you had in mind?

To return to the exit, turn to page 54.
To step into the water, turn to page 58.

"Sorry guys," you say. "I think this is as far as we go. Thanks for bringing us, but Tonya and I need to be heading back."

Ines gives you a concerned look. "Are you sure you can make it back on your own?"

You glance over your shoulder. It was a pretty straight shot. You don't think it'll be any problem getting back to the manhole. "We've got it," you say. "Don't worry."

She shrugs. "Well, nice to meet you. Enjoy the rest of your trip."

You watch and the three of them disappear around a corner. Their lights slowly dim, and then fade away. You and Tonya are alone. The realization sends a chill up your spine.

"Let's get out of here," you say. You make your way through the tunnel, retracing your steps. Soon, you come to a fork. Tonya starts down one tunnel while you move for another.

"Wait a second," she says. "It was this one."

"No, it was that one," you insist. You shine your lights down both passageways, but both just lead into darkness.

"Look," you say, sighing. "We can't be far from the exit now. Why don't we each go a little way down the tunnel we think is the right one. If we see the exit, we'll shout."

Tonya makes a face. "Split up? Is that really a good idea?"

To agree with Tonya and stay together, turn to page 63.

To split up and search for the exit, turn to page 65.

"Well, if you're not worried, then I'm not either," you say. "Let's keep going."

As you move deeper into the maze of tunnels, you get a greater sense of the age and size of the catacombs. You try to imagine what it must have been like for those who built them so long ago.

Few changes have been made to the catacombs since they opened to the public in 1809.

The ceiling looms closer and closer. You can touch it with the palms of your hands in some places.

"What's this?" René says, coming to a stop. He shines his light on a pile of broken stone. "This wasn't here last time."

"Maybe this was the noise we heard," Tonya says.

Peter scratches his head. "I guess so. Interesting. Collapses in the catacombs are rare, but they do occur."

René moves his light up to the tunnel's ceiling. There's a thin, jagged crack. A cloud of dust slowly seeps out of the crack.

"We should get out of here," Tonya whimpers.

To look closer at the crack, turn to page 72.

To run, turn to page 74.

You've come this far. Why stop now? You hand your phone to Ines for safekeeping. Then you follow Peter into the water. The cold water almost takes your breath away.

You swim until you hit a wall. "Now what?" you ask. "We can't go any farther."

René smiles. "The tunnel probably rises ahead. If it didn't, there wouldn't be water here. Let's see if we can make it to the other side."

With a deep breath, you dive under the water and start to swim. You keep a hand on the wall as you go, not wanting to lose your bearings. You count as you swim . . . *20 . . . 21 . . . 22*. There's no end in sight. Panic starts to set in. You keep counting . . . *30 . . . 31 . . . 32*. You can't go much farther. You're going to need air!

To turn around, turn to page 68.

To press on ahead, turn to page 70.

You give the tunnel one last look, then shrug your shoulders. "You're right, Tonya," you say. "We'll just stick with the tour."

You spend the rest of the afternoon glued to Louis's side. He tells the group how old the catacombs are and how they became a mass grave in the late 1700s. The skulls start to seem almost friendly.

Too soon, you're back up to the surface. You're a little disappointed, knowing that you only saw a tiny fraction of what lies beneath the ancient city. But then your stomach rumbles. You and Tonya head off to your next adventure—to try a Parisian crepe. Soon, your very safe and ordinary trip into the catacombs is just another memory of Paris. Maybe you'll return one day.

THE END

To follow another path, turn to page 9.
To learn more about the Paris Catacombs, turn to page 103.

You still regret not going with Ines and the other cataphiles.

"Sorry, I just want to take a quick look," you say. Tonya stares at you with a scowl on her face.

You slide through the gate and make your way down the corridor. It's narrow here. You have to walk with your shoulders slanted forward just so you don't scrape against the rough walls.

The light ahead is dim, but it's definitely there. It grows brighter as you get closer. It's a solid light with a slight blue cast. It captures your attention—so much so that you stumble over a crack in the corridor's floor. Your body lurches forward, but you catch yourself before you fall. You take a deep breath in relief. That was close. You can see how easily someone could fall and get hurt down here.

You make your way around a slight bend in the corridor. Suddenly you see the source of the light. It's a flashlight resting on the corridor floor. Its cone of light illuminates a shape—it's a young woman. She's lying on the ground. For a moment you fear she's dead. Dried blood mats her hair and face. But as you peer at her face, you can see that she's breathing.

The single public entrance to the catacombs is in Paris's 14th district.

Turn the page.

"Hello," you say gently, touching her arm. She stirs and opens her eyes. Her gaze is glassy.

"Help," she says in a raspy voice. "I . . . I fell."

You waste no time running back into the ossuary. You spot Louis and call out for him. He springs into action, calling for help. Soon, emergency teams arrive with a stretcher.

"She'll be OK," says one of the EMTs. "She's lucky you found her though. If she'd been down there overnight, who knows what would have happened. This is why people should never wander off alone into the catacombs."

He's right. It was a bad idea to stray from the group. But for the woman's sake, you're sure glad that you did.

THE END

To follow another path, turn to page 9.
To learn more about the Paris Catacombs, turn to page 103.

Tonya has always had a better sense of direction. One time you actually got lost inside an art museum trying to find the bathroom. Maybe it's best just to trust her. "Fine, lead the way," you say with a huff.

The two of you continue your careful crawl along the passageway. Your feet are soaked and you're shivering. You've never wanted to see the sky as much as you do now.

You're starting to feel crushed. The walls seem very, very close. Panic is setting in. "We're not going to find it!" you shout. "Help! Help! Someone help us!"

Tonya grabs you. "Stop it!" she shouts. "Look!" she points straight ahead. You can barely see it. A glow. Your eyes widen. It's daylight!

Turn the page.

You hurry along toward the light. As the two of you emerge from the catacombs, you feel the weight has been lifted off of your shoulders. You breathe deeply.

Your adventure in the Paris Catacombs is over. You don't think you'll go underground any time soon.

THE END

To follow another path, turn to page 9.
To learn more about the Paris Catacombs, turn to page 103.

"It's not really splitting up," you say. "I mean, it's just for a minute. See if you can spot anything. Then we'll both come right back here."

Tonya reluctantly agrees. She starts down her passageway as you make your way slowly down yours.

"See," you shout. "We can even talk to each other as we go."

"What?" she calls back. You can barely make out what she's saying. It's more of an echo.

It's just for a minute, you remind yourself again. You keep moving, sweeping your flashlight back and forth as you move. You scan for any light ahead, but you can't make out anything.

"How am I supposed to see daylight with this flashlight on?" you mutter to yourself. You click off the light for a better look.

Turn the page.

Darkness seems to drop around you like a heavy veil. Sounds seem louder and farther away. Even though you can't see the walls, they seem closer than ever. There's not a hint of light in any direction. You turn around, searching for any glow. But there's nothing.

You reach toward your pocket for your flashlight. You fumble for it, and it falls to the ground. You can hear the crack of plastic breaking. You drop to all fours, pawing the damp floor. Finally, you find the flashlight. Just by feel, you know it's beyond repair.

Panicked, you rise to your feet. You don't know which direction you're facing. Which direction leads back to Tonya? You're confused. You can barely move.

"Help! Help! Help!" you shout. But the only sound you can hear is your own voice echoing back at you.

Go back the way I came, you think. You're not sure if what's behind you is the right way. But you can't just stand there. As you turn, your foot catches a crack in the floor. You wave your arms, trying to catch yourself as you fall, but it's no use. Your head hits the ground with a thud.

When you wake up, you have no idea how much time has passed. Has it been a minute? Has it been hours? There's no way to know. You're lost and alone. Will Tonya find you down here? Or will the Catacombs of Paris add one more set of bones to their countless millions?

THE END

To follow another path, turn to page 9.
To learn more about the Paris Catacombs, turn to page 103.

You can't risk going farther. You flip yourself around and start kicking back in the direction you came. But you're swimming blind. You swim headfirst into a wall. You flip again, kicking for all you're worth . . . *52 . . . 53 . . . 54.*

BAM! You slam into another wall. You can feel the tunnel's ceiling above you. There's no way to get air. Your lungs are burning. You want to scream, but you know you can't. If you open your mouth, water will rush into your lungs.

Suddenly something grabs your ankle. It pulls you, dragging your body along the ceiling. Just when you can't hold your breath any longer, you're out. You gasp for air as Tonya helps you out of the water.

"You were thrashing all around," she says. "I had to pull you back!"

You throw your arms around your sister. "You saved my life!" you say.

A few moments later, René's head pops out of the water. "We found the way through," he says. "Come on!"

"No thanks," you say, wringing out your shirt. "We've had our adventure for today. You guys go ahead. We're headed back to the exit. Thanks for everything."

Part of you will always wish you'd seen what was on the other side. It's a lifelong regret. But mostly, you're just glad to have escaped the catacombs of Paris with your life.

THE END

To follow another path, turn to page 9.
To learn more about the Paris Catacombs, turn to page 103.

Just a little farther, you tell yourself. You push forward, keeping a hand on the wall. You keep counting . . . *43 . . . 44 . . . 45*.

Suddenly, you're through. You take a deep breath. Tonya pops up behind you a second later. René, Peter, and Ines are hollering and giving each other high-fives.

"What's going on?" you ask. "Did I miss something?"

"This is completely unmapped!" Peter says, waving his phone in the air. "There's no record of this area being explored before. It's possible we're the first people to stand in this tunnel in more than a thousand years! Can you imagine?"

Ines takes careful measurements of the tunnel on her phone as Peter snaps pictures.

"OK," Ines says. "Time to go back."

Some tunnels are sealed with concrete. This stabilizes the ground above and also keeps out explorers.

"But aren't we going to explore more?" you ask.

Peter puts a hand on your shoulder. "We have to record this before we go deeper. It's a major find. We can't risk getting lost down here. Then no one would ever know about this new network of passages."

"Maybe you can come back with us tomorrow," Ines says, smiling.

You can hardly wait.

THE END

To follow another path, turn to page 9.
To learn more about the Paris Catacombs, turn to page 103.

"That's strange," you say. You rub your fingertips along the edges of the crack. "Is it normal for the tunnel to be . . ."

A huge chunk of ceiling comes off in your hand. Bits of debris crumble off, falling down your shirt sleeves and bouncing off your face. You try to wipe the dust away from your eyes. As you lean over, another piece of ceiling hits you in the back of the head.

The ceilings in some areas are very low.

Tonya pulls you to safety. Your eyes clear just in time to see a massive wall of stone collapse, blocking your exit.

But that's not the worst news. As you explore your surroundings, you find an even larger pile of broken stone blocking the path ahead. You are trapped. Your light is running out. Cell phones get no reception down here. And although the cataphiles insist that people know they've gone into the tunnels, there's no way anyone knows exactly where you are.

Your adventure into the Catacombs of Paris will not have a happy ending.

THE END

To follow another path, turn to page 9.
To learn more about the Paris Catacombs, turn to page 103.

"Run!" you shout. Without a moment's hesitation, you all turn and dart back the way you came. The group's shouting and footsteps are quickly drowned out by a thunderous boom that fills the tunnel. It's caving in!

Plumes of dust shoot through the stale air as countless tons of rock come crashing down. You can feel the rush of air from the falling debris. But you're lucky. You manage to stay just ahead of it. You run, and you don't stop running until the cave-in is far behind you. The five of you finally come to a stop, huffing for air as you lean against the tunnel walls.

"That . . . that was too close," Ines says, shaking. The rest of you are quick to agree. "We have to get out of here in case there's more. Everyone, follow me."

You follow Ines as she quickly navigates back to the surface. When you finally poke your head out into daylight, you breathe easy for the first time since the collapse. The five of you sink down onto the ground and begin to laugh.

Your adventure into the catacombs will be one you never forget. As you look back on it, you realize it was a terrible, reckless idea to venture down there without a guide. But the memories— and friends—you made will last a lifetime.

THE END

To follow another path, turn to page 9.
To learn more about the Paris Catacombs, turn to page 103.

Chapter 4

TO THE RESCUE

It's a relaxing afternoon in Paris. You're sitting in a cafe, enjoying a coffee and watching the people of the city walk by. You've got nothing planned for the day. It's a rare chance to relax, and you're going to take full advantage of it. Everything is setting up for the perfect afternoon.

That is, until your friend Pierre shows up. His face is bright red, and he's breathing heavily.

"What's wrong, Pierre?" you ask.

He takes a moment to catch his breath. "We have a problem," he says. "Ines and some tourists are missing. They went down into the catacombs a few hours ago. We haven't heard from them since."

Turn the page.

Your heart immediately starts pounding. Pierre's news is shocking. Ines is a fellow cataphile. You're a small, tight-knit community who shares a common interest. You delve down into the Catacombs of Paris to map and explore the city's underground tunnels—even the ones that are off limits to the public.

You've been in the caves with Ines many times before. She's smart and careful. If she hasn't checked in, that means there's something wrong.

"Let's go," you say. "I'll need to stop for my gear."

Pierre shakes his head and lifts a backpack. "There's no time. I've got everything we need. I know where she was exploring yesterday. The entrance isn't far from here."

You and Pierre weave through the bustling streets. He veers off into a series of little-used alleyways and heads to a manhole. The manhole cover is moved to the side.

"That's got to be where they went in," Pierre tells you.

The two of you put on your gear. Despite the warm weather, you slip into a light jacket—the underground catacombs can be chilly. You lace up a pair of waterproof boots. You check the two flashlights Pierre hands you. One is your primary light and one is a backup. You never, ever go into the catacombs without a backup light.

"Let's go," Pierre says.

Usually, trips below ground come with a sense of fun and adventure. Not today. Today, you're all business. Ines might need your help.

Turn the page.

The two of you lower yourselves down the manhole using a series of rungs built into the concrete. After a short climb, you drop down into the catacombs. Your feet hit the stone floor with a plop and a splash. It's been raining, which means that everything will be damp and slick.

Exploring the catacombs outside of a tour has been illegal since 1955.

You move down a straight passageway. After a short walk, it forks in two directions. You shine your light into both tunnels. You don't see any signs telling you which way Ines went. Cataphiles take pride in leaving no traces behind. Preserving the catacombs is one of the most important parts of what you do.

"Which way do we go?" Pierre asks. "Should we split up?"

Normally, you'd reject splitting up. It's dangerous to venture alone into the catacombs. But this is an emergency. Every second counts. Is it OK to do it, just this once?

To stay together and choose a passageway, turn to page 82.

To split up and cover more ground, turn to page 85.

You quickly dismiss the idea of splitting up. "No, we can't do that," you say. "The last thing we need is two more people in need of rescue. If we're going to do this, we do it right. We do it safely."

"I've never used this entrance before," Pierre says. "Have you?"

"No," you answer. "I just found out about it from Ines a few days ago. I wonder if it links up to the entrance the police sealed off a few months ago."

Your group is always on the lookout for new ways to access the catacombs. The police seal any new entrances as soon as they can. That's why most cataphiles are so tight-lipped about where they can get in. And it's why you were surprised to hear that Ines was bringing a couple of outsiders in with her.

Some of the tunnel walls are covered in graffiti. You frown at it. The brightly colored spray paint ruins the mysterious atmosphere of the catacombs. You pass an intersection littered with soda cans and candy-bar wrappers. Teenagers like to come down here to party sometimes. Their litter makes you even angrier. Without even thinking about it, you pick up the trash. You will throw it away later.

You work your way through a narrow passage. In some places, it's so tight that you have to walk sideways to squeeze through.

"What's that?" Pierre asks. He points his beam of light at a pile of loose rocks lying on the tunnel floor ahead. You just shrug your shoulders. You're in a mine. Piles of rocks aren't unexpected.

Turn the page.

As you continue, though, you see more and more rubble on the floor. Down here, there's no telling if it's been there a day or a century. But something seems unsettled.

That's when you hear a groaning noise. It sounds like rock scraping against rock.

"What was that?" Pierre asks.

"Whatever it is, it can't be good," you reply. "I'm not sure we should be down here."

"But if something's wrong, Ines needs us more than ever," Pierre argues.

To continue on, turn to page 89.
To turn back and head for the surface, turn to page 98.

Time could be critical. You need to cover as much ground as you can. You bend your safety rules just this once. "You go that way," you say, pointing to the right. "I'll go this way. Be safe."

At one point, there were 300 known entrances to the catacombs. Many have been sealed, but new doors are being opened all the time.

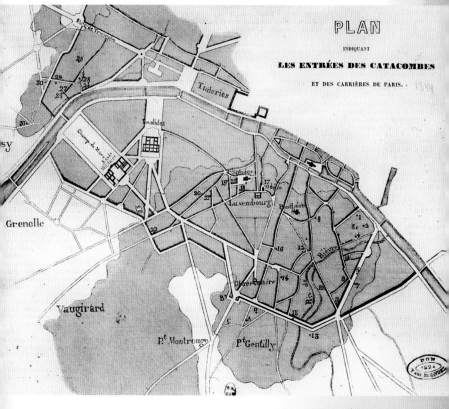

PLAN
INDIQUANT
LES ENTRÉES DES CATACOMBES
ET DES CARRIÈRES DE PARIS.

Turn the page.

You watch as Pierre's light disappears down the passageway. Then, with a deep breath, you head the opposite direction. You've never gone into the catacombs alone before.

The tunnel narrows. Soon it's so tight that you have to walk with your shoulders at an angle. When the tunnel finally opens up again, you're met with a solid rock wall. It's a dead end!

Or is it? Before you turn around, you notice a small opening near the floor. You might be able to squeeze through. Ines definitely could have.

To turn around, go to page 87.

To try to squeeze through the opening, turn to page 91.

You might be able to fit through the opening, but it would be a big risk. It's better to turn around and check in with Pierre.

You've always felt comfortable in the catacombs. But now, alone, you feel uneasy. A quick glance at your watch shows you that you've been down here for half an hour. You've got another 30 minutes or so of battery left in your primary flashlight. Once that's gone, you'll only have your backup. You'll have to head back to the surface. You don't want to be caught down here in the dark.

Your boot slips on the wet, slick tunnel floor. You fall fast and hard. As you flail your arms, your flashlight flies out of your hand. It hits the floor just a second after you do. The light blinks and dies.

Turn the page.

You groan, rubbing your head and backside. Everything hurts. With your light out, the catacombs are pitch black. You sit there for a moment in the darkness with your head throbbing.

What's that? Did you hear something? You strain to listen. Was it a voice? It's so faint that you could have imagined it.

You reach into your pocket and grab your backup flashlight. Could Ines be calling for help?

To head back to meet Pierre, turn to page 94.

To search for the noise deeper in the catacombs, turn to page 96.

Pierre is right. Time is critical. You need to keep going as fast and as safely as you can.

The passageway dips, leading you deeper and deeper into the catacombs. "Would Ines have gone this far?" Pierre asks.

You've known Ines for years. She's a good explorer, but she's a bit reckless. You sigh.

Turn the page.

The average temperature in the catacombs is 57 degrees Fahrenheit (14 degrees Celsius.)

"Yes," you say. "She might have. Let's look for another five minutes. If we don't find anything, we'll head back."

You don't need five minutes though. The tunnel before you has collapsed. A massive pile of jagged rock blocks your way.

"Wow," Pierre says. "I've never seen a collapse like this before. It looks recent."

Now what do you do?

To give up the search and turn around, turn to page 98.
To try to get past the rubble, turn to page 100.

"Ines!" you shout. "If you're there, I'm coming!"

The opening is just big enough to fit through. You lie flat on the wet tunnel floor and go feet first through the rectangular opening. You push your legs through, then force your torso. Finally, you raise your arms over your head and give a strong push, hoping to feel the tunnel open on the other side.

But that doesn't happen. Instead, the opening narrows sharply. It feels as if part of the stone above you has collapsed.

"No!" you shout. Now you'll never be able to make it through. You'll just have to go back the way you came and continue your search somewhere else. You push off your feet to go back through the opening.

Turn the page.

But you don't move. Your boot is caught in a crack. You pull. You wiggle your foot. No luck. You try to pry your foot free of the boot. Nothing works—it's wedged too tight. You feel cold sweat on your face. The more you struggle, the more trapped you feel.

The skeleton of Death guides tourists through the Paris Catacombs in a print made in 1816.

"Help!" you cry. "Heeeeeeelp!"

The minutes tick by. Your flashlight dims, sputters, and then finally dies. You can't reach your backup light in your pocket. It wouldn't do you any good if you could. You're trapped.

You can only hope Pierre calls the police for help. It's what you should have done in the first place.

THE END

To follow another path, turn to page 9.
To learn more about the Paris Catacombs, turn to page 103.

You take a long look back down the tunnel. You can't hear anything now. It could have been your imagination. The darkness, along with a knock on the head, could leave anyone hearing things.

"No," you say out loud, hoping that the sound will reassure you. "I've got to head back."

You pick yourself up. Your pants are soaked from the wet tunnel floor. You're cold, sore, and still just a bit woozy from the fall. You put your hand on the tunnel wall to steady yourself as you head back.

You keep your eyes and ears open the rest of the way. You don't see any sign of Ines and her group. You have little trouble navigating your way back to the exit. You've spent enough time down here. You wait until Pierre returns.

"No luck?" you ask. He shakes his head. You sigh. You don't have much choice now. "Let's go up," you say. "We'll call the police. They've got dogs trained to sniff out survivors. They'll have a far better chance finding Ines than we do."

You try to sound hopeful. But you know the truth. When someone is lost in the catacombs of Paris, there's a real chance he or she will never be found.

THE END

To follow another path, turn to page 9.
To learn more about the Paris Catacombs, turn to page 103.

Your head is swimming from the fall. You know that you're in no condition to go deeper into the catacombs. But you thought you heard something, and you have to be sure.

As you head deeper into the tunnel, you pause to listen. You think you hear the voice again. Or was it just dripping water? You have to know. You press on, deeper and deeper. You come to an intersection. Someone has spray-painted a skull and crossbones on the tunnel walls.

Vandals, you think, annoyed. They're the reason these parts of the catacombs are off limits. It doesn't occur to you that the painting could mean anything else. As you go deeper, your light begins to flicker. That means you've been down here for almost an hour.

"Just a little farther," you whisper to yourself. You beg your flashlight to hold out.

The flashlight begins to dim, but it doesn't go out. It does do a poor job of showing you the way, though. As you hurry on, you don't see that the tunnel leads to one of the large wells that falls straight down into the quarries. One moment you're trotting along through the passageway. The next, you're falling! You bounce off of sharp, jagged rocks.

The landing will not be soft. You know that the Paris Catacombs has claimed one more soul.

THE END

To follow another path, turn to page 9.
To learn more about the Paris Catacombs, turn to page 103.

You don't like this. You sweep your flashlight back and forth. Dust is heavy in the air. Down here in the catacombs, dust tends to settle. If it's in the air, that means it's recent. And from the sounds you just heard, you're afraid the ceiling could collapse at any moment. Even a loud noise could cause a cave-in.

The catacombs are full of sculptures and carvings made by workers over the years.

"We've got to get out of here," you whisper.
Pierre takes a long, hard look, but he has no
choice but to agree. The two of you turn around
and hurry back to the surface. As you emerge
into the light of day, you feel a heavy weight
on your shoulders. You will call the authorities
in hopes they can find your friend. But you
can't shake the feeling that when you left the
catacombs, you were also saying goodbye.

THE END

To follow another path, turn to page 9.
To learn more about the Paris Catacombs, turn to page 103.

Every instinct tells you to run. But you can't bring yourself to leave. What if Ines is on the other side of the rubble?

"Ines!" you shout. "Ines!"

Silence. Pierre's breathing is the only sound you can hear. Then you hear it. A muffled voice, soft and distant. "Help! We're trapped!"

You look at Pierre. His eyes are wide.

"Ines!" you shout together. "We're coming!"

You start moving the pile of rubble out of the way. The stone is heavy, and it takes both of you to move the biggest pieces. Thirty minutes pass. Then an hour. Your primary flashlights dim and die. You work by the glow of Pierre's backup light, saving your own for the journey back up.

Finally, you break through. Pierre's light shines through a small opening to the other side. "We're here!" he calls. "Just hold on!"

You paw at the opening until it's large enough to crawl through. You help pull Ines and four others through. They've got cuts and bruises, and they're covered in dust, but otherwise they're OK. You wrap Ines up in a big bear hug.

"I thought we were dead," Ines says, sobbing.

"You're not," you answer. "But we all will be if we don't get moving. We're down to one flashlight."

It's a frantic trip back to the surface, but you make it. Daylight has never looked so good.

THE END

To follow another path, turn to page 9.
To learn more about the Paris Catacombs, turn to page 103.

Chapter 5

EMPIRE OF THE DEAD

Few places in the world are filled with as much wonder—and terror—than the Paris Catacombs. It's a maze of more than 200 miles (322 kilometers) of underground passageways that travel far beneath the city streets. The tunnels, which were dug for mining limestone, are at least one thousand years old.

It wasn't until the late 1700s that the catacombs earned their nickname: The Empire of the Dead. At the time, Paris was facing a crisis. The city's graveyards were overfilled. Old graves were being dug up to make room for the newly dead. Bones were stacked on top of each other inside the cemetery walls.

In 1780 heavy rains caused one of the city's main cemetery walls to collapse. Corpses spilled out onto the streets. Something had to be done.

Paris did not have to look far to find a place for its dead. The ancient quarries and tunnels underneath the city seemed like the perfect final resting place for more than 6 million people. It was a massive effort to dig up and move the bodies. It started in 1785 and continued on and off until about 1814. Many of the bones laid there are arranged in ornate patterns, decorating walls and columns.

Since then, the Paris Catacombs have remained a curiosity to some and a fascination to others. They opened for public viewing in 1874. The tunnels have hosted explorers, filmmakers, ghost hunters, thieves, and soldiers. Today, firefighters use them to practice rescue missions.

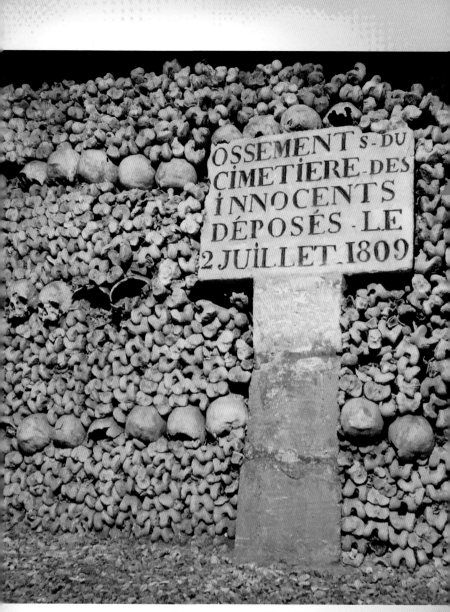

Bones are arranged based on the cemetery they came from.

The bones in the ossuary were arranged as a way to bring in tourists. It worked. The first people to explore with a guide arrived in 1967. Since then, hundreds of thousands of visitors come to admire the walls famously lined with skulls and bones.

The catacombs have given rise to the strange culture of the cataphiles. These enthusiasts delve into the depths of the catacombs, exploring and mapping the seemingly endless network of tunnels and ossuaries. Their work is illegal but also important.

Exploring in the dark isn't without risk. Pits, mine shafts, and wells—with and without water—can all be found in the tunnels. And not all the water is clean or safe. Although many paths have been mapped and recorded, others remain a mystery.

It's little surprise that the catacombs have claimed their share of victims. One wrong turn can leave an explorer hopelessly lost. One missed step can lead to a disastrous fall. One stroke of bad luck can leave explorers trapped alone in the dark. The catacombs are a strange and dangerous place, but they're also full of wonder.

TRUE STORIES OF THE PARIS CATACOMBS

1783: Philibert Aspairt, the doorman at a Paris hospital, entered the catacombs. Legend says he was searching for a treasure trove of wine hidden in the tunnels. He was not found until 1804, and by that time it was too late. The ring of keys on his belt was the only thing left to identify. He was just a few steps away from an exit.

1939–1945: During World War II, German troops occupied Paris. Some citizens formed a secret resistance to the enemy German army. Resistance fighters often used the catacombs to move around the city and avoid German detection.

2004: Police found a small cinema set up in one of the catacombs' off-limits chambers. There were carved stone benches for 30 people and included a bar, restaurant, private rooms, and a bathroom. When authorities returned a few days later, the cinema was gone. All they found was a note that read, "Do not try [to] find us."

2016: Thirty-year-old Alison Teal of Hawaii brought her surfboard into the flooded chambers of the catacombs. Teal became the first person to surf through the world's largest grave.

2017: Thieves made their way through the catacombs to pull off a stunning heist. From the depths of the catacombs, they drilled into a wine cellar and stole about 300 bottles of high-priced, vintage wine.

2017: Two teenage boys wandered into the catacombs. They quickly became lost. They survived three days in darkness, suffering from hypothermia, or low body temperature. Rescue workers and dogs found the boys and brought them safely to the surface.

OTHER PATHS TO EXPLORE

◈ Many people look at the ossuaries as a work
of art, with their carefully arranged skulls and
other bones. But some argue that each of those
bones represents a real person, and that using
their remains in art is disrespectful. How might
you feel if you knew someone would one day use
your bones in art? Would you be OK with it?

◈ Cataphiles have formed their own society
that centers on the catacombs. They are very
secretive. Some don't even use their real names
while underground. How might a cataphile feel
about outsiders coming to the secret tunnels
that they love?

◈ The citizens of Paris faced a crisis in the late
1700s. They had nowhere to bury their dead.
As bodies stacked up, it became a health
crisis. Eventually, workers brought the bodies
underground at night. Why do you think they
did this? As a citizen of Paris, would you have
objected to the work being done during the day?
Why or why not?

READ MORE

Hyde, Natalie. *Ancient Underground Structures.* Underground Worlds. St. Catharines, Ontario; New York: Crabtree Publishing, 2019.

Roza, Greg. *Ossuaries and Charnel Houses.* Digging Up the Dead. New York: Gareth Stevens Publishing, 2015.

Winterbottom, Julie. *Frightlopedia: An Encyclopedia of Everything Scary, Creepy, and Spine-chilling, from Arachnids to Zombies.* New York: Workman Publishing, 2016.

INTERNET SITES

The Catacombs of Paris
https://www.cometoparis.com/paris-guide/paris-monuments/the-catacombs-of-paris-s955

The Paris Catacombs
http://www.catacombes.paris.fr/en

The Unbelievable Story of the Paris Catacombs
https://www.walksofitaly.com/blog/paris-catacombs

INDEX